Reading Pádraig Ó Tuama's marvellous new book is like living inside a prayer. Consoling and inviting, challenging and inspiring, his beautiful meditations and luminous prayers will help you reflect more deeply on God's poetic action in your life.
James Martin SJ, author of *Jesus: A Pilgrimage*

You hold in your hand a month's worth of recipes for spiritual nourishment. They are simple: it will only take a few moments to prepare your heart to make room for them. They are deep: as soon as you have used them for a month, you will want to begin again because each reading invites you deeper. I've never seen a book of prayers like this one. I think this is just what my soul needs.
Brian D. McLaren, author of *The Great Spiritual Migration*

In this beautiful collection of simple lucid prayers Pádraig Ó Tuama invites us to lay our trinkets aside and turn to our treasure. And this anthology is indeed a treasure: prayers that turn hostility towards hospitality, prayers that help us say what we mean and not we thought we were meant to mean. This book will help any reader to be 'honest to God', and in that honesty, encounter afresh the love that casts out fear. Each of these prayers offers a rich, poetic response to the words of Jesus, utterly free of cant and religious jargon, a surprising and refreshing companion for all of us on the Emmaus Road.
Malcolm Guite, priest, poet, author *Parable and Paradox*

Oh I need this book of prayers! They find me where I am, and as I am – alive, human, exiled – and resuscitate an ancient way to a true reconciliation within myself, with others, and with a power greater than myself. I do not need to be ashamed. The stones over which we stumble can be made into altars. And Jesus is returned to me as a person of presence and imagination, able to listen and to heal by his close attention – a living guide to the power of radical love.

Marie Howe, State Poet of New York (2012–2014)

When the merest mention of religion and politics hints at hopelessness and hostility without end, *Daily Prayer from the Corrymeela Community* offers us a way forward, conjuring a healing space in which to be human together. As Pádraig Ó Tuama sees it, to pray is to imagine, to take up the art that names our desires, our confusions and curiosities, and gives them form. This collection invites us to experience old rhythms as fresh revelations and new language as deeply in sync with ancient life-giving witness.

David Dark, author of *Life's Too Short To Pretend You're Not Religious* and a professor of religion and literature in Nashville

Daily Prayer

with the Corrymeela Community

Pádraig Ó Tuama

CANTERBURY
PRESS

Norwich

© Pádraig Ó Tuama 2017
First published in 2017 by the Canterbury Press Norwich
Editorial office
3rd Floor, Invicta House
108–114 Golden Lane
London EC1Y 0TG, UK

www.canterburypress.co.uk

Canterbury Press is an imprint of Hymns Ancient & Modern
Ltd (a registered charity)

Hymns Ancient & Modern® is a registered trademark of
Hymns Ancient & Modern Ltd
13A Hellesdon Park Road, Norwich,
Norfolk NR6 5DR, UK

British Library Cataloguing in Publication data

A catalogue record for this book is available
from the British Library

978 1 84825 868 6

Typeset by Manila Typesetting Company
Printed and bound in Great Britain by
CPI Group (UK) Ltd

Contents

Do mo PD
agus
mo thuismotheoirí, Paddy agus Ann,
le grá agus buíochas don scáth.

Oremus

A few years ago, at Mass, I was sitting near a woman who had a small boy on her lap. He looked to be about three years old. It was an ordinary Sunday mass and the child seemed like an ordinary child. At the time of consecration, the faithful were quiet, the bell was rung, the priest held up the sacrament and everything was as expected. Then the child, who had, up to now, been quiet, shouted out:

'Hello Jesus!'

He dragged out the hello into one long yodel. Helloooooooooooo. Everybody in the church turned.

Like many children, he knew an audience when he had one, so he lauded out the louder:

'Helloooo Jesus!'

It was a moment of delight. The priest looked shocked, blank, as if Jesus had turned up, in the actual flesh and bone. Shut the child up, you could hear in the fear. Theologically, of course, the child was deliciously correct. The woman holding the small boy looked mildly embarrassed but mostly thrilled. I cannot remember anything else from that mass apart from the warm welcome of a small child who took the story seriously; the small child whose words of welcome were the surprise of praise among the predictable.

I'm guessing he'd been told to say hello to Jesus around the time the bell tolls. He hadn't yet learnt the difference between inner voice and outer voice. But who among us learn this? So he greeted: loudly, warmly, with a welcome as wide and magnificent as the world.

It can be a shock to take Jesus of Nazareth seriously.

It can be difficult too, whether seeking Jesus during a sacrament or trying to find conversation between your story and the story of a son of Mary: he was such a particular man, with interests in words and power and tables and edges; with interests in theology and leadership and food and friends. He lived during a time of occupation, during a time of expectation, during a time of intensity. Many have been living in his wake since.

So much of the life of Jesus is hidden: his walks to the wilderness; his early mornings; the shape and smell of his body; the sound of his voice; the words he said underneath his breath; the sound of his voice; the sound of his breath. He sometimes lifted up his own voice in joy and praise, like that small boy in Mass. When he died, he prayed the night-prayer from the place of torture. 'Into your hands,' he said, reciting from the twenty-second psalm, words that many said at night. In his prayer, we hear the interplay between form and freedom, and the space between them; the ways in which form and freedom feed each other, helping us enjoy the art of prayer when the art is available; helping us put old rhymes to our cries when the art of life seems cruel.

I have heard it said that 'Prayer is not an art. It is a cry.' I liked that thought for a while, especially when I thought that form was a form of constriction, that the breath of prayer needed to be free.

But breath has form. In fact, breath *is* form, the fundamental rhythm by which we live, and breathe and have our being. God's breath is over the chaotic waters, we read. Our breath is in the chaotic body and, we hope, might have a touch of the holy about it too.

Breath, like prayer, is a cry. Breath, like prayer, can also be an art. Prayer is a small fire lit to keep cold hands warm. Prayer is a practice that flourishes both with faith and doubt. Prayer is asking, and prayer is sitting. Prayer is the breath. Prayer is not an answer, always, because not all questions can be answered.

Prayer can be a rhythm that helps us make sense in times of senselessness, not offering solutions, but speaking to and from the mystery of humanity. Growing up, our family said a decade of the Rosary in Irish every night. We would name our requests – a sick friend at school; an exam; a dying member of the family – I hated it. It was a good thing and I hated it. I hated it because I was a teenager and because destruction is attractive, and because the form and art of the rosary seemed removed from the devices and desires of a teenager. I perfected the art of pretending to be asleep. I practiced the art of disdain. It was, in its own way, its own cry – defiant then, understandable now.

When I moved out of home, I bought little wooden beads, I bought some string, and a friend gave me a beautiful copper cross. I made rosary beads and now, the art of them sustains me – the touch, the texture, the repetition of words. I can still only pray the Rosary in Irish. The rhythm of those words, *Sé do bheatha a Mhuire*, is a shelter, a support, and the form gives sound to times when other things fail.

These are some of the things that prayer is. Prayer is rhythm. Prayer is comfort. Prayer is disappointment. Prayer is words and shape and art around desperation, and delight and disappointment and desire. Prayer can be the art that helps you name your desire. And even if the desire is only named, well, naming is a good thing, surely. Naming is what God did, the Jews tell us, and the world unfolded. Or perhaps naming is what the Jews did, and God unfolded. Either way, I'm thankful. Naming things is part of the creative impulse. Naming the deep desires of our heart is a good thing, even if those desires are never satisfied.

No prayer is perfect. There is no system of prayer that is the best. There is only the person praying, the person kneeling, the person walking with beads between their fingers, the person cursing God, or gloom, or fate, or whatever it is that seems to be not listening. Henri Nouwen said that the only way to pray is to pray; the only way to try is to try. So the only way to pray well is to pray regularly enough that it becomes a practice of encounter. No prayer is hollow – whether it is answered in one way or the silent way. To name the night is to be like God, speaking light to formless voids, putting rhythm and rhyme to the pell-mell that compels us. To pray is to trace the edge of chaos and find a way to contain it, not control it. Even if the story we pray to is only a fiction, it might be fiction that'll save us. Or it might change us. To pray is to imagine. And in imagining, we may imagine that we are imagined by something Bigger. The Zulus sometimes call God *uNkulunkulu*, Big-Big. My friend Emma calls God the Bigness, or sometimes, The Smallness. God of Gods. Light of Lights. Story of Stories. In whom our own chaos and creation are contained. Holy Holy Human.

Ignatius, the salty saint of the imagination, had a solution for days when the day escaped you. He suggested a small examen, a ten-minute reflection where you begin with connecting with the source of all Goodness, and then tell yourself the story of your day before noting the consolations and desolations, the uplifting moments and the pitfalls of the day before then preparing for the next day. Even the uncontained can be a container for the rhythm of hope.

I remember talking to Ignatius one time when my own life felt like it was falling apart. He had given advice about how to live a life and I was trying to live a life with his advice in mind. I wrote prayers down in a small book. It wasn't working and I thought Ignatius was being an idiot. I told him. And in the telling, I heard a question and an opening into a new conversation. I remember I told him about a road that was filled with wet leaves and graffiti and I was broke and broken, and the prayer didn't change much, but the conversation was good. I still re-read those arguments and marvel at the echo chamber that kept me, if not safe, then safe enough; if not unafraid, then unafraid enough.

If we are going to take Jesus of Nazareth seriously, we must take him in truth. In Irish, if you want to say seriously, you say *i ndáríre*, which might mean something like 'in truthfulness'. So we take the truthfulness of a man born in a time of occupation seriously; we take the truthfulness that all human lives needed warmth, changing, touch, love and loneliness to flourish; we take the truthfulness of ignorance seriously. And to take Jesus of Nazareth seriously, we must take ourselves seriously. It's no use trying to pretend to be him. We are not him. He is not us. But the Christian hope says that he was among us, and he looked out for the people who caught his attention. So I think we must pay attention: to ourselves; to our hate; to our deepest yearning; to our abandonments; to our creativity; to our edges; to our endings; to our violences and voices.

The first 31 collects in this book are reflections on the life of Jesus, weaving in and out of the injunction to not fear. They are the gospel texts that the Corrymeela Community reflects on in our small book of prayer. All kinds of people in all kinds of circumstances with all kinds of reasons to be afraid are told not to be afraid. They probably were afraid. But their fear, like our fear, could be a beginning of courage.

The collect has beautiful form, like a haiku of intention. It has five folds. The person speaks to God; the person names part of the story of God; the person names their desire – only one desire; and then the person praying gives a reason why this is the one desire they name. This fourth fold echoes the first two: the name and the named story of God. And then the person finishes their prayer – with an Amen, or with a small bird of praise.

Almighty God, to whom all hearts are open, and all desires known. You know this prayer. It is a collect. It names God, and then tells some of the story of God and us. It unfolds a petition: *Cleanse the thoughts of our heart:* this is our desire. And this is why: so that our love may be better than it is now, a little bit less imperfect, because we need it, because without love, what are we? *We ask this in the name of the one who named the world.*

Why do we move toward rhythm? Perhaps it's because the first thing we hear – the first thing we feel, it's the same thing – is the heartbeat. Perhaps it's because the breath works on form, perhaps it's because we discover ourselves when we change a form. We need something to hold and something to hold us and something that tries to hold us back – form works, form tells truths, form helps us to be, in and out of form, in and out of season.

And the form of prayer, like the form of poetry, can be local too. In Irish poetry, one finds an *Aisling*, a poem where the ghost of a woman wakes a slumbering poet and laments for her lost lover. The ghost is a country and the lover is the help that never helped. A Japanese Haiku interplays seventeen syllables with an elegance of thought with an underpinning of nature. A sonnet has fourteen lines and a volta to heal and hurt the world.

At one point, Jesus turned to his disciples and said 'What were you arguing about along the way?' The story unfolds. They have been arguing about power and privilege, prowess and other words beginning with *p*. From an argument about power, Jesus sits down. Responding to men's talk about power, Jesus brings a child into the room, holds the child and speaks about welcome. To reflect on this every day for a life would be a life well lived. The particular form of prayer can be the entrance to participating in a small mystery. We do not need to practice every kind. We need to practice a kind of prayer that works and keep practicing. Seek the way that works, Ignatius says. So this book has a few ways that might work. If they don't, even better. Prayer discovers its own vernacular.

What is the form of prayer for conflict? It is sometimes elegant, sometimes ragged. It is sometimes silent, and sometimes the repetition of a story until the story doesn't need to be repeated any more. Corrymeela was begun by Rev. Ray Davey, together with some students from Queen's University in Belfast, in 1965. These were the days before the Troubles broke out, but the days when troubles were brewing. Questions about jurisdiction of Northern Ireland captivated the political imaginations of individuals, and neighbourhoods – already divided – deepened their divisions. People died. People were frightened. There was a need for a place of friendship, a soft place for hard conversations, a meeting place where hostilities could be explored within the context of hospitality.

This place was Corrymeela, a small Irish cliff with a view to Rathlin Island and Scotland. Ray raised money, and a plot of land on the north coast of Antrim was bought: six acres of lumpy land with an old house and a view to live for. The land itself breathes, the land is a sacrament, and a balm for troubled tales about jurisdiction.

From its beginning, Corrymeela has welcomed people who bring their differences on pilgrimage with them. At Corrymeela, we do not seek to undo differences, merely we hope and pray that we can learn to hold our differences differently. Some people come for a weekend retreat, some come for a week, some join the community holding to a simple rule of life to find moments of reconciliation in the ordinary and extraordinary moments of the everyday. We believe that the complication of civic, religious and political life is best explored in community: in the gathered space of cups of tea; shared meals; fireplaces; discussions; debates; disagreements; arguments where we hope we can find new ways to name old pains. Listening is a sacrament when the topic is important, and when strife divides people in small places, the sacrament of listening is vital. So many people and so many places in the world have difficult relationships with difference. We seek to practice the art of hospitality in the places of hostility, and in so doing practise kindness in places most in need of kindness.

Corrymeela employs people to run programmes and events that explore what reconciliation can look like in our troubled, healing, stitched and changing society. We rely on over 80,000 volunteer hours per year. We work with about 10,000 people each year and we also are supported by the members of the community – those individuals who weave the commitments of Corrymeela into their homes and work. Corrymeela's commitments are simple: we hold doubts and faiths together; we are shaped by the witness of Jesus who uncovered the hollow heart of victimization; we meet for residential weekends of learning, worship and community; we give time, skill and finances to support the work; we confess that we are part of the problems of division and we work hard to be part of the solution; and, finally, we pray.

We have a small prayerbook where, each day, we read the names of members of the staff, volunteers and community. We have some intentions in prayer and we reflect on a text. Each day – from 1 to 31 – has a gospel text, and the corresponding entries in this book of prayer offer prayers and reflections on those texts. Joining with us in these days is joining with a hope, an essay, a breathing practice in the simple integration of reconciliation with the everyday. The tradition of Corrymeela is Christian. It is from Christian hope and Christian harm that our witness comes, and to be faithful to our voices of complicity and consolation, we speak from the voice of Christianity. This can be a tense stance; so much pain has come from this particularity of following God and the sacred story. But this, too, demonstrates the artistic dilemma of form, and the hope that working within form, one might find within it the breadth of the world. So we are a Christian community with space at the table, working hard to make our Christian witness a welcoming one. If poetry is to be universal, Robert Frost said, it must be parochial. It's the same for us: our parish is a Christian story, our hope is the story of the wild and wonderful world.

When I was lonely and living in the French-speaking part of Switzerland, I went to a Latin mass accidentally. I got talking to the priest afterwards and it was immediately clear that we could become friends. He invited me to his house for white wine that tasted of fresh apples, we made home-made fondue and he spoke beautifully in a language I stumbled through. It was in these masses that I learned to love the sung *Oremus* that calls the faithful and the tired to prayer. *Oremus* means 'Let us pray.' That style of mass surprised me, I was minded to hate it, but I found comfort there. It is so particular, so formal, so rigid. The Latin word *oro*, from which *oremus* comes, refers, in the first instance, to mouth, and has flavours of Hittite, Greek and Sanscrit lurking in it, like a smirk at the corner of particularity. From across languages and traditions, continents and doctrines, Language speaks: Open your mouths, sinners and saints, and pray.

Corrymeela means 'Lumpy Crossing Place'. Initially, when the community was founded, somebody said that it meant 'Hill of Harmony', but they were wrong, and I'm glad. Places of need are full of stones. We stumble. We work hard to harvest. We can make shelters and art from the rocks that we stumble over. Our practice is exactly that – a practice. We practice the art of paying attention to the hostilities of our day; we make a rhythm of texts that hold a world of pain and hope; we weave our stories of pain into a hope that we might live well together; we practice the habit of prayer.

We turn to prayer in days of joy, and days where our world shows – again – that it is wrapped in a circle of conflict. We turn to form, we turn to old words because sometimes it is old words that hold the deepest comfort and the deepest challenge. We turn, with one intention, to the particular experience. Like the beloved pilgrims wandering the sands between Egypt and the Promised land, we, together with the collect, learn from the deep intention and name God from that intention. So in a time of trauma, God is given a name by the traumatized. In a time of joy, God is named by the joy of our hearts. In a time of confession, God is named as light. In a time of rest, God is the soft dark that enfolds us. It can be difficult to speak of God, and so we turn with joy to the meat of God in the body of Jesus: in his arguments, anxieties and aspirations, we find contradictions and counterpoints to our own; in his pleasures, pains and praises we hear echoes of a life lived seriously.

Sometimes prayer is a comfort. And sometimes that's enough. And sometimes it works. Once, I was sitting with more zeal than sense in a church, praying with fervour for something like holiness, or righteousness, or some other term I still don't understand. All of a sudden, the question came: *What do you actually want?* I was shocked by its clarity. It was a blunt question, one that demanded truthfulness, not devotion. I couldn't answer. I got up, I walked out. The prayer came with me. I'm still answering it.

Prayer, like poetry – like breath, like our own names– has a fundamental rhythm in our bodies. It changes, it adapts, it varies from the canon, it sings, it swears, it is syncopated by the rhythm underneath the rhythm, the love underneath the love, the rhyme underneath the rhyme, the name underneath the name, the welcome underneath the welcome, the prayer beneath the prayer.

So let us pick up the stones over which we stumble, friends, and build altars. Let us listen to the sound of breath in our bodies. Let us listen to the sounds of our own voices, of our own names, of our own fears. Let us name the harsh light and soft darkness that surround us. Let's claw ourselves out from the graves we've dug, let's lick the earth from our fingers. Let us look up, and out, and around. The world is big, and wide, and wild and wonderful and wicked, and our lives are murky, magnificent, malleable and full of meaning. Oremus. Let us pray.

How to use this book

I have always wanted to write a book of recipes. Soups, probably; something to warm the heart. My recipes are vague about amounts but come with poetry suggestions. When cooking stew, for instance, it is best to read Patrick Kavanagh's *In Memory of My Mother* (both versions, check out Tom Stack's edited collection) aloud; when making roast pear, chicken and garlic soup (topped with blue cheese) it is always wise to read Marie Howe's *Magdalene – the Seven Devils*; and when you mix red onion, with red peppers, fresh tomatoes and fresh strawberries, topped with a suspicion of chilli, lime, basil and saltflakes, you should always, and only, read Mary Karr's *Disgraceland*. If you're putting roast butternut squash in a soup with coconut milk, make sure to toast pine nuts, and top the soup with those and a little sesame oil. Read Seán Ó Riordáin's *Oidhreacht Fán Anam* while you do it, it'll break your heart. You'll need to learn Irish first, but everything good requires effort. Alternatively, listen to Íarla Ó Lionaird's sung version with The Gloaming.

My friend Devin phoned me from California once wanting to know whether a recipe I'd written required one clove of garlic or two. He was asking the wrong person, but he was a man in need of detail and he believed that I loved him enough to give him detail even if I didn't have detail to give. How many do you feel you need? I asked him. He laughed and called me an idiot. He asked me again, how many cloves of garlic? Use your imagination, I said, but he wanted to use mine. I love him dearly, so I made an answer up. It worked, I think. I forget how many cloves.

Most of us are in a dialogue when we read a book. I know I am. That's the point, I think; to listen to the writer, to listen to yourself and to listen to the space between where things said by neither are nonetheless said. The things we take away are the things that we were already looking for. *What you seek is seeking you*, said Rumi, and while this is a frightening concept, it can a consoling one if we listen to the desires that will feed us, not destroy us. Rumi asks us to trust that wisdom waits, and might be found in unlikely corners.

So read a lot, make pots of soup and use this book however you want. Mix up the prayers, and make your own. Write in the margins, cross words out, fix them, make a solution.

Sometimes I pray the morning prayers and then turn to the day of the month for a text and a collect, and then add in intentions of my own, finishing with the Prayer for Courage. Courage is the mixture between fear and resolution, and only exists when we do something about it. Do not fear, we hear over and over. The prayers in this book are prayers that start with the fear and move toward the doing. Do not *only* fear, we say. It's a fine beginning, let courage be your moving. Let prayer help.

Ignatius of Loyola said: 'That level of prayer is best for each particular individual where God our Lord communicates Himself more. He sees, he knows, what is best for each one and, as he knows all, he shows each the road to take. What we can do to find that way with his divine grace is to seek and test the way forward in many different fashions, so that an individual goes ahead in that way which for him or her is the clearest and happiest and most blessed in this life.'

All of that goes to say: you'll need to make your own damned soup, because only you can make it. You know your own needs, or you will. Take bones and flesh and blood and fruits of the dark earth, put in water, put in salt and put a fire to it. Let it boil, let it cool a little. Season with what your season needs. Eat it, drink it, survive and look around. Be a little bit glorious. Be warm and open. Share. Keep some for tomorrow. Give plenty away. Amen.

MORNING, MIDDAY
AND EVENING PRAYERS

Morning prayer

We begin our day alone,
honouring this life, with all its potentials and possibilities.

We begin our day with trust,
knowing we are created for loving encounter.

We begin our day with hope,
knowing the day can hold
love, kindness,
forgiveness and justice.

A reading followed by a time of silence

We recall our day yesterday,
May we learn, may we love,
may we live on.

We make room for the unexpected,
May we find wisdom and life
in the unexpected.

Help us to embrace possibility,
respond graciously to disappointment
and hold tenderly those we encounter.
Help us be fully present to the day.

A short silence

We pray for all whose day will be difficult,
May we support, may we listen,
may we change.

We resolve to live life in its fullness:
We will welcome the people who'll be part of this day.
We will greet God in ordinary and hidden moments.
We will live the life we are living.

A short silence

May we find the wisdom we need,
God be with us.

May we hear the needs of those we meet,
God be with us.

May we love the life that we are given,
God be with us.

Prayer for courage

Courage comes from the heart
and we are always welcomed by God,
the Croí[1] of all being.

We bear witness to our faith,
knowing that we are called
to live lives of courage,
love and reconciliation
in the ordinary and extraordinary
moments of each day.

We bear witness, too, to our failures
and our complicity in the fractures of our world.

May we be courageous today.
May we learn today.
May we love today.
Amen.

Amen.

---

1 *The Irish word Croí (pronounced 'Kree') means 'heart'
and is the name for the chapel space in Corrymeela, a beautiful circular place of prayer, built into the ground, with a living
roof and echoes. In the Croí, we have prayers, we had dia-
logues, silence, and our morning and evening liturgies.*

Midday prayer

We break from the doings of our day
and make space to notice you.
You are always with us
in surprising guises.

Jesus of the flesh, we meet you in
worker and friend,
stranger and pilgrim,
the needy and the needed,
the questioner and questioned.

So when we meet you,
may we deepen trust,
deepen life, deepen justice
and deepen joy.

And when you meet us,
help us approach our activities
with presence and power,
with love and humility,
with courage and dignity.

Amen

Prayer for Courage (see page 5)

Evening prayer

We reflect on the day:

For the love shared
we are grateful
For provision and nurture
we are grateful
For kindness given
we are grateful.

For the sorrow we've caused,
we pray for forgiveness
For injustices ignored,
we pray for forgiveness.

For the encounters with God today, in stranger and friend,
We bid you welcome.
For the encounters missed today,
We know that you always see us
even when we don't see you.
For tomorrow,
May we see you
in ways expected and unexpected.

We welcome the dark of the night.
We make space for it, and we mark our place in it.

We remember that you, Jesus of Nazareth,
lived through nights of consolation and desolation.

And you walked into the nights of those people you met
inviting them to justice and truth, love and life.

We welcome the night,
and we welcome you into all our nights.

We pray for those who work by night,
whose day is marked by moon, cloud and stars.

And we pray for those whose nights are desolate,
that they may have the consolation of prayer,
peaceful solitude and community.

For a peaceful night,
we pray.
For a hopeful day,
we pray
For a deeper generosity,
we pray.

Prayer for Courage (see page 5)

Amen.

Day 1

But the angel said to them, 'Do not be afraid; for see – I am bringing you good news of great joy for all the people.'

Luke 2.10

God of fear,
God of the night,
God of the expectation,
You visited shepherds in the night
with songs and sights of joy.
In all of our nights, turn us
towards hope, because
hope might just
keep us alive.
Amen.

Day 2

Then Joseph got up, took the child and his mother by night,
and went to Egypt.

God of Exile,
You were carried into Egypt
by people fleeing danger.
We pray for all in exile
that they, like you, can find home
and shelter and safety.
Because you were exiled
and you remain with
the exiled.
Amen.

Day 3

'This is what the Lord has done for me when he looked favourably on me and took away the disgrace I have endured among my people.'

Luke 1.25

God of Elizabeth,
When Elizabeth heard news of joy,
she celebrated
not because she was part of an important story
but because a kind story
had wrapped itself around her,
and the disgrace she had endured
was lightened.
Lighten the places of our disgraces. Lighten them.
Wrap yourself and your story around us.
Because you can be the great story
that surrounds us.
Amen.

Day 4

'He has shown strength with his arm; he has scattered the proud in the thoughts of their hearts. He has brought down the powerful from their thrones, and lifted up the lowly.'

Luke 1.51–52

God of Mary, Son of Mary:
Neither birth nor death diminished you.
Neither power nor pain destroyed you.
Neither plenty nor little distracted you.
So lift up our arms in strength
so that we may lay down
our arms and our armies,
our fears and our prejudices.
Because, with Mary, we know that
the silenced have words to speak
Amen.

Day 5

'By the tender mercy of our God, the dawn from on high will break upon us, to give light to those who sit in darkness and in the shadow of death, to guide our feet into the way of peace.'

Luke 1.78–79

God of promises,
Sometimes we wait generations
for the dawn from on high;
sometimes only years.
We wait for justice and hope and light and kindness
to mingle in the tangle of our days.
And we age while we hope.
So may we age and hope
with tenderness and truth.
Because you are tender and true
even though we sometimes wonder.
Amen.

Day 6

They said to him, 'Rabbi, where are you staying?' He said to them, 'Come and see.'

John 1.38–39

Jesus of Nazareth,
You met unlikely people in unlikely places
and joined yourself to them in friendship.
May we be like you in this way,
finding friends at crossroads and bus-stops,
in queues and crises, in kindness and curiosity.
Because we, like you,
need the company of others.
Amen.

Day 7

Then Levi gave a great banquet for him in his house; and there was a large crowd of tax collectors and others sitting at the table with them.

Luke 5.29

Jesus of the table,
You gathered unexpected people around
hearths of hospitality.
You stretched out your hand
for grapes and bread, for wine and welcome.
May we populate our tables
with all kinds of people.
Because at the table
our hearts can be glad
for a while.
Amen.

Day 8

Leave your gift there before the altar and go; first be reconciled to your brother or sister, and then come and offer your gift.

Matthew 5.24

God of Reconciliation,
You demand much of us –
inviting us to tell truths
by turning towards each other.
May we leave our trinkets where they belong
and find our treasure
by turning towards each other.
Because you needed this.
Because we all need this.
Amen.

Day 9

They came to Jesus and saw the demoniac sitting there, clothed and in his right mind, the very man who had the legion; and they were afraid.

Mark 5.15

God of the Edges,
even muzzled fear growls,
you know this.
You saw this in the people who had chained
the man who howled.
Open in us a thousand thousand pathways
into story.
Because you did this, and Hell was emptied.
Amen.

Day 10

But the woman, knowing what had happened to her, came in fear and trembling, fell down before him, and told him the whole truth.

Mark 5.33

Jesus, our intuitive brother,
Your body told you that somebody had touched you.
She had touched you with courage
pushing past bodies to reach you.
May we push past and make way.
May we tell the whole truth and listen
Because you were arrested by this woman
whose tortured story
changed you.
Amen.

Day 11

Then turning toward the woman, he said to Simon, 'Do you see this woman? I entered your house; you gave me no water for my feet, but she has bathed my feet with her tears and dried them with her hair.'

Luke 7.44

Jesus of Nazareth,
Strangers came to you
because, with you,
they hoped that they'd be seen
for who they were
not for who the seers saw.
May we who are strangers see each other,
because we, like you,
need to be seen to be believed.
Amen.

Day 12

'Why do you call me "Lord, Lord", and do not do what I tell you? I will show you what someone is like who comes to me, hears my words, and acts on them.'

Luke 6.46

Jesus,
You praised work more than words,
foundations more than fashion.
May we find our foundation
in the work of Love;
demanding, tiring,
true and human and holy.
Because Love is the only foundation
worth building on.
Amen.

Day 13

For truly I tell you, whoever gives you a cup of water to drink because you bear the name of Christ will by no means lose their reward.

Mark 9.41

Jesus our rewarding friend,
You knew need.
You knew thirst and hunger.
And so do we.
We praise and honour
the surprising providers
of comfort and care.
We praise and honour them.
May their work increase.
We praise and honour them
because without them
we thirst.
Amen.

Day 14

'Am I not allowed to do what I choose with what belongs to
me? Or are you envious because I am generous?'

Matthew 20.15

Jesus, our generous
and upsetting
friend,
You gave freely,
even when this caused pain to those who loved you.
May we see beyond our envy,
to the generosity that wove
and wounded you.
Because anything less
will fail us,
like it failed you.
Amen.

Day 15

When Jesus realized that they were about to come and take him by force to make him king, he withdrew again to the mountain by himself.

John 6.15

Jesus,
You sometimes left
so that people could face themselves.
May we face our
selves,
in the wilderness and the world,
and recognize
the forces that drive us,
so that they do not always drive
us.
Amen.

Day 16

An argument arose among them as to which one of them was the greatest. But Jesus, aware of their inner thoughts, took a little child and put it by his side, and said to them, 'Whoever welcomes this child in my name welcomes me.'

Luke 9.46–48

Jesus of the Way,
When your friends argued
about power and prestige
you stood someone
unnoticed by them all among them
and spoke of welcome.
May we who are powerful
look beyond our power;
may we who are unnoticed
be noticed;
may we find the welcome
that waits for us.
And in so doing
welcome you
who welcomes us.
Amen.

Day 17

One of his disciples, Andrew, Simon Peter's brother, said to him, 'There is a boy here who has five barley loaves and two fish. But what are they among so many people?'

John 6.8–9

God of the barley loaf,
God of the boy,
God of the fish,
And God of the humble brother;
When we do not have enough,
may we use what we have
to do what we can.
Because a small boy did this,
and generosity listened.
Amen.

Day 18

When Jesus came to the place, he looked up and said to him, 'Zacchaeus, hurry and come down; for I must stay at your house today.' So he hurried down and was happy to welcome him.

Luke 19.5–6

God who made trees and bodies,
God who made the ground and grand gestures,
May we practice happy hospitality,
because here,
hostilities can be healed.
Amen.

Day 19

The dead man came out, his hand and feet bound with strips of cloth, and his face wrapped in a cloth. Jesus said to them, 'Unbind him, and let him go.'

John 11.44

Lazarus, silent brother of Bethany,
When you died, they washed and wrapped you.
And when you came back they unwound you,
and you washed yourself.
In all of this, you said nothing.
We, like you, are silent in the face of death.
But may we wash and wrap love around sorrow
Because sometimes, that's all that we can do.
Amen.

Day 20

He got up from the table, took off his outer robe, and tied a towel around himself. Then he poured water into a basin and began to wash the disciples' feet and to wipe them with the towel that was tied around him.

John 13.4–5

Uncovered Jesus,
You washed
the feet of your friends
with your hands.
We do not know what to do
with this kind of love
or this kind of power
so we repeat it once a year.
May we repeat it more often:
every month; every day; every hour; every encounter.
Because this is how you chose to show
love and power
to your friends.
Amen.

Day 21

While they were eating, he took a loaf of bread, and after blessing it he broke it, gave it to them, and said, 'Take, this is my body.'

Mark 14.22

Jesus,
When you had nothing else to give
you gave yourself.
And as your friends shared and ate,
they were confused and complicit,
just like all of us.
May we give – our lives and confusions;
our hollowness and our hearts –
because when we give like this,
we are like you,
who became like us.
Amen.

Day 22

'This is my commandment, that you love one another as I have loved you. No one has greater love than this, to lay down one's life for one's friends.'

John 15.12–13

Jesus,
We only know the names
of some of your friends.
Not all.
But we know some of the names
of all of ours.
May we love them well:
with time and thanks;
with welcome and warmth;
with strength and kindness.
Because this, this, this,
is great love.
Amen.

Day 23

Then Jesus said to him, 'Put your sword back into its place; for all who take the sword will perish by the sword.'

Matthew 26.52

Jesus of the sheathed sword,
in your name, many swords have been used
and many people have perished.
Speak to us, teach us, again and again,
that violence begets violence.
Teach us. Again and again.
Over and over.
Because we keep forgetting,
and we need to keep
remembering.
Over and over.
Amen.

Day 24

So Pilate, wishing to satisfy the crowd, released Barabbas for them; and after flogging Jesus, he handed him over to be crucified.

Mark 15.15

Gods of Pilate,
you are loud and lazy,
following the fashions of the day
making lies out of love
and making mockeries of meaning.
And – so often – we follow you.
May we instead, follow that small whisper,
even when we barely hear it,
even when we barely believe it,
even when it hurts.
Because this is what love is.
This is what love is.
Amen.

Day 25

Then he said, 'Jesus, remember me when you come into your kingdom.' He replied, 'Truly I tell you, today you will be with me in Paradise.'

Luke 23.42–43

Dying Jesus,
at the end of yourself
you turned,
and spoke words of
togetherness
in the places of the torn.
May we always find
words to hold,
especially in times
when the world
harms.
Because sometimes
words can
heal.
Amen.

Day 26

'Peace I leave with you; my peace I give to you. I do not give
to you as the world gives. Do not let your hearts be troubled,
and do not let them be afraid.'

John 14.27

Jesus, you shared peace
around a table of anxiety,
peace with the bread, peace with the wine,
peace in the face of the uncertain,
peace in the place of pain.
May we share tables of peace
in places of pain,
sharing food and friendship
and words and life.
Because you came to a fearful world
and found your place
around those tables.
Amen.

Day 27

When Judas, his betrayer, saw that Jesus was condemned, he repented and brought back the thirty pieces of silver to the chief priests and the elders. He said, 'I have sinned by betraying innocent blood.'

Matthew 27.3–4

Judas, sainted scapegoat,
When you saw that your friend was condemned,
you repented
and ended yourself.
We pray for all
who are on the edges of themselves.
We pray that they may not be alone.
We pray that they may not betray their deepest dignity.
Because God gathers all
in the boughs of the beloved.
Amen.

Day 28

But the angel said to the women, 'Do not be afraid; I know that you are looking for Jesus who was crucified.'

Matthew 28.5

Jesus of the cold grave,
pilgrim women followed you
in life and in death.
Bless all pilgrims who bring life
to the places of the dead.
Because they are the unafraid.
Amen.

Day 29

Now it was Mary Magdalene, Joanna, Mary the mother of James, and the other women with them who told this to the apostles. But these words seemed to them an idle tale, and they did not believe them.

Luke 24.10–11

Surprising Son of God
you revealed the truth to women
who were not believed by men.
You are in the voices of the unbelieved
and the ignored.
So bring us towards each other.
Bring us towards
the truest truth.
Because here, if anywhere,
will we find you.
Amen.

Day 30

They said to each other, 'Were not our hearts burning within us while he was talking to us on the road, while he was opening the scriptures to us?'

Luke 24.32

Hidden Jesus,
Wandering along the way
like a stranger,
hidden along the way
in many stories and many faces.
May we listen to our hearts
when they burn with life
knowing that you are speaking to us.
Because you are with us
along the way
in the faces
of many strangers.
Amen.

Day 31

When it was evening on that day, the first day of the week, and the doors of the house where the disciples had met were locked for fear, Jesus came and stood among them and said, 'Peace be with you.'

John 20.19

Jesus,
our dead and living friend,
We walk the ways of death and life
holding fear in one hand
and courage in the other.
Come find us when we are locked away.
Come enliven us.
Come bless us with your peace.
Because you are the first day of creation
And all days of creation.
Amen.

PRAYERS FOR TIMES
OF DIVISION

A prayer in times of violence

God of all humanity,
in times of violence
we see how inhuman we can be.

We pray for those who, today, are weighed down by grief.
We pray for those who, yesterday, were weighed down by grief.

And the day before,
and all the days before the day before.

We pray, too, for those who help us turn towards justice and peace.

Turn us all towards justice and peace
because we need it.

Amen.

A prayer for groups

God of groups,
You are within and beyond all of our borders:
our names for you; our words about you; our gatherings;
our stories about you.

We seek to praise but sometimes we imprison.

May we always be curious about what is beyond borders,
going there gently, knowing you have always been there.

We ask this because we know that
you are within
and beyond
all our groups and our stories.

Amen.

A prayer for reconciliation

Where there is separation,
there is pain.
And where there is pain,
there is story.

And where there is story,
there is understanding,
and misunderstanding,
listening
and not listening.

May we – separated peoples, estranged strangers,
unfriended families, divided communities –
turn toward each other,
and turn toward our stories,
with understanding
and listening,
with argument and acceptance,
with challenge, change
and consolation.

Because if God is to be found,
God will be found
in the space
between.

Amen.

A prayer of shelter and shadow

Ar scáth a chéile a mhaireas na daoine.
~ It is in the shelter of each other that the people live.
~ It is in the shadow of each other that the people live.

We know that sometimes we are alone,
and sometimes we are in community.

Sometimes we are in shadow,
and sometimes we are surrounded by shelter.

Sometimes we feel like exiles –
in our land, in our languages and in our bodies.
And sometimes we feel surrounded by welcome.

As we seek to be human together,
may we share the things that do not fade:
generosity, truth-telling, silence, respect and love.

And may the power we share
be for the good of all.

We honour God, the source of this rich life.
And we honour each other, story-full and lovely.

Whether in our shadow or in our shelter,
may we live well
and fully
with each other.
Amen.

Prayers in times of change

God of Yesterday,
we knew you then:
your promises; your words;
your walking among us.
But yesterday is gone.
And so, today, we are in need of change.
Change
and change us.
Help us see life now
not through yesterday's stories
but through today's.
Amen.

God of Endings,
What we thought would not end
has ended.
And we find ourselves here
wondering where we are
and how we got here
and where to go
from here.
Be with us, here, at the end.
Help us place our feet on this ground
help us lick our wounds,
help us look up and around.
Help us believe
the story
of today.
Because you know all

about the endings
of today.
And you are not afraid.
Amen.

Changing God
You changed your mind.
And we, too, change our minds
about you.
We want to change
toward
the better.
Change with us
because
we know
you want to.
Amen.

Prayer for a new name

So she named the Lord who spoke to her, 'You are El-roi';
for she said, 'Have I really seen God and remained alive after
seeing him?'

Genesis 16.13

God of Hagar,
When Hagar was exiled in the desert
she met you
and gave you a name:
the Living One
Who Sees Me.

We have walked far,
and have seen many things
and now,
because of what we have seen
because of where we are going
because of where we are
we give this new name now.

We do not destroy past names,
because they have brought us here.

We celebrate the new name
that will bring us on.

Because you are known by many names –
names which bring us on.

Amen.

Prayer for resilience and repentance

From there he set out and went away to the region of Tyre. He entered a house and did not want anyone to know he was there. Yet he could not escape notice, but a woman whose little daughter had an unclean spirit immediately heard about him, and she came and bowed down at his feet. Now the woman was a Gentile, of Syrophoenician origin. She begged him to cast the demon out of her daughter. He said to her, 'Let the children be fed first, for it is not fair to take the children's food and throw it to the dogs.' But she answered him, 'Sir, even the dogs under the table eat the children's crumbs.' Then he said to her, 'For saying that, you may go–the demon has left your daughter.' So she went home, found the child lying on the bed, and the demon gone.

Mark 7.24–30

Jesus of Nazareth,
When you met the
woman of Syrophenicia,
you called her a little dog
but that didn't stop her.
Little dogs need little crumbs,
she said,
and you listened,
repented,
and praised her for her words.

We praise her words too,
and ask that that we can speak like her,
and listen like you.
Because this is the gift of
resilience
and repentance.
This just might save us.
Amen.

STATIONS OF THE CROSS

1 – Jesus is condemned to death

God of the accused
and the accusing,
who made the mouths, the ears and the hearts
of all in conflict.
May we turn ourselves towards that
which must be heard,
because there we will hear your voice.
Amen.

2 – Jesus takes up the cross

Burdened God,
who bore the weight of wood
on torn shoulders,
We pray for the torn and the burdened,
that they may be held together by
guts and goodness.
Because you were held together
by guts and goodness.
Amen.

3 – Jesus falls for the first time

God of the ground,
whose body was – like ours – from dust,
and who fell – like we fall – to the ground.
May we find you on the ground
when we fall.
Oh, our falling fallen brother, may we find you,
so that we may inhabit
our stories,
our selves.
Amen.

4 – Jesus meets his mother

Mary, Mother of Failure,
You met your son at the end,
in a place beyond words,
and must have felt faithless
and empty and alone.
We pray that we may have the grace
to live with our own
stories of failure,
knowing that love can continue
even when things end.
Amen.

5 – Simon of Cyrene helps Jesus to carry the cross

Simon of Cyrene,
stranger from afar,
You were a help
to an unknown man.
We pray for all who help:
that their help may be helpful;
that their kindness may be kind.
Because yours was,

even though you knew
you couldn't do
enough.
Amen.

6 – Veronica wipes the face of Jesus

Veronica,
your story is doubted
but valuable.
You did what you could
even though it was very little.
May we do the same
even when we doubt.
Amen.

7 – Jesus falls the second time

God of the Fall,
You felt the fall
when your body fell to the ground
a second time.
Gather all who fall.
Gather all our fallings.
Gather the voices.
Gather the breath that's
forced from our bodies.
Because falling, too,
has a story.
Amen.

8 – Jesus meets the women of Jerusalem

Women of Jerusalem,
while you mourned,
Jesus saw you
and spoke to you –

he in his sorrow seeing you in yours.
May we see each other,
even when we feel unseen.
Because when we see each other,
we are seen ourselves.
Amen.

9 – Jesus falls the third time

Jesus of the dirt,
you were led to death
because of how you lived.
Help us live like this;
walking and falling, and walking
and falling,
like you,
in the ways of the living
and the dead.
Amen.

10 – Jesus is stripped

Jesus of the flesh,
Naked you came from the womb
and naked you were made for the cross.
What was designed
for indignity and exposure
you held
with dignity and defiance.
May we do the same
Because you needed it
Because we need it.
Amen.

11 – Jesus is nailed to the cross

Jesus of Nazareth,
This cross was a torture.
It only gives life
because you made it hollow.
Bring life to us, Jesus,
especially when we
are in the places
of the dead.
Because you brought life
even to the instruments of death.
Amen.

12 – Jesus dies on the cross

Jesus of the imagination,
You never grew old, always a young man,
and most of us grow older
than you did.
When lives are cut short
the living question the meaning of living.
May we live with meaning,
even when meaning fades,
making meaning
so that we
have something to live for.
Amen.

13 – Jesus is placed in the arms of his mother

Mary, Mother of Death,
You held the corpse of your young son
– the worst of fears –

in your arms,
as he went where we have not yet gone.
We mark this
with silence and art.
May we also learn from fear,
because fear
won't save us from anything.
Amen.

14 – Jesus is placed in the tomb

Jesus of the unexpected,
for at least some of your life
this was not how you imagined its end.
Yet even at the end,
you kept steady in your conviction.
Jesus, keep us steady.
Jesus, keep us steady.
Because, Jesus, keep us steady.
Amen.

Stations of a story

The fourteen stations of the cross are found in most Catholic churches. While in some countries they are represented by fourteen single crosses, they are most often represented by fourteen images that give stopping-points, or stations, in the journey from the condemnation of Jesus of Nazareth to his death by Pontius Pilate, the prefect of the Roman province of Judea from AD 26–36.

These stations were not fixed, however. Over centuries, some were added, others were removed and regional differences existed, too. Even today, we note that some churches may add a fifteenth station – a station of resurrection – to their devotion, and since Pope John Paul II, it has been popular for ecumenical services to explore what are popularly (and clumsily) called 'The Biblical Stations'.

All of this points to a need in people to put chapters and stopping points to stories of devotion and meaning. To freeze the frame like this helps the person to put themselves at the heart of a text, or in an unnoticed corner of a text, or an ignored point of view. By taking a gospel text and putting personal stations to it, a dialogue between reader and story takes place and something called prayer emerges in the thin place between reader and read. There we encounter the heart. There we meet the place of projection, and the place where the wisdom we didn't know we had can greet us. There we can greet the truth that a story can hold us. There we can greet that which we call God.

And so, as an example, the final chapter of John's gospel could be stationed like so:

- Peter decides to go back to fishing.
- Six of his friends come with him.
- They spend the night on the boat.
- They catch nothing.
- A stranger calls to them from the shore and they answer.

And so on.

Or, we could take the story – from either Matthew or Luke – of Jesus' encounters with temptation in the desert.

- Jesus is compelled to go to the desert.
- Jesus spends his first night alone in the desert.
- Jesus is hungry.
- Jesus wonders what to do.
- Jesus wonders how to live with who he is.
- Jesus is tempted to take a short cut to satisfaction.
- Jesus turns to scripture.
- Jesus is tempted to abuse power for his own gain.
- Jesus turns to prayer.
- Jesus is tempted to follow.
- Jesus turns to hope.
- Jesus is comforted.
- Jesus returns to his friends.
- Jesus waits to be tempted again.

To engage with the text this way requires careful and heartfelt reading, noticing the nooks and crannies where the imagination can lodge, paying attention to the curiosities that emerge and creating a stopping-point there. In so doing, a new story emerges, the story of rhetoric between the text and the reader. Unexpected moments have the light of your attention shone on them, the story changes, we change, we find a new way into an old story. This is a work of theology. It is also a work of intelligence. And it is a work of prayer.

God of the story,
You are in and out of the stories we read
calling us into them
and calling us out of them.
Give us courage to listen to our own curiosities
as we read old stories.
Dare us to ask the questions
hidden in the heart of the text.
Lead us to mine – with heart and mind
and desire and desperation –
the many meanings
in the one story.
Because this is where we find you
and where you
find us.
Amen.

LITURGY OF MORNING
AND NIGHT

A liturgy of the morning

On the first morning God said: 'Let there be birds.' And God separated voice from voice; and in some voices, God put a song, and the song sang to the land, and to the light, and to the light on the land, and when the people heard it, the morning had begun. The first morning. **And God said that it was Good.**

And on the second morning God said: 'There will be dreams from the night that will need the light of the morning.' And so God put wisdom in the early hours. The second morning. **And God said that it was Good.**

And on the third morning, God said: 'Let there be a certain kind of light that can only be seen in the morning.' And God created gold, and dew, and horizons, and hills in the distance, and faces that look different in the light of the morning, and things that look different in the light of the morning. The third morning. **And God said that it was Good.**

And on the fourth morning, God said: 'Sometimes the day will be long. Let there be a warmth in the morning, let people sleep for some mornings, and let the rest of the morning be good. The fourth morning. **And God said that it was Good.**

And on the fifth morning, God said: 'There will be people who will rise early every morning, whose day will begin in the night, by the light of moon and stars; they will see the sun rise, these early risers. And God put a softness at the heart of the dawn. The fifth night.
And God said that it was Good.

And on the sixth morning, God listened. And there were people working, and people struggling to get out of bed, and there were people making love and people making sandwiches. There were people dreading the day, and people glad that the night was over. And God hoped that they'd survive. And God shone light, and made clouds, and rain, and rainbows, and toast, and coffee, places to love the light and places to hide from the light. Small corners to accompany the lonely, the joyous, the needy and the needed. The sixth morning.
And God said that it was Good.

And on the last morning, God rested. And the rest was good. The rest was very good.
And God said that it was very Good.

A liturgy of the night

On the first night God said: 'Let there be darkness.' And God separated light from dark; and in the dark, the land rested, the people slept, and the plants breathed, the world retreated. The first night.

And God said that it was Good.

On the second night God said: 'There will be conversations that happen in the dark that can't happen in the day.' The second night.

And God said that it was Good.

And on the third night, God said: 'Let there be things that can only be seen by night.' And God created stars and insects and luminescence. The third night.

And God said that it was Good.

And on the fourth night, God said: 'Some things that happen in the harsh light of day will be troubled. Let there be a time of rest to escape the raw light.' The fourth night.

And God said that it was Good.

And on the fifth night, God said: 'There will be people who will work by night, whose light will be silver, whose sleep will be by day and whose labour will be late.' And God put a softness at the heart of the darkness. The fifth night.

And God said that it was Good.

And on the sixth night, God listened. And there were people working, and people crying, and people seeking shadow, and people telling secrets and people aching for company. There were people aching for space and people aching for solace. And God hoped that they'd survive. And God made twilight, and shafts of green to hang from the dark skies, small comforts to accompany the lonely, the joyous, the needy and the needed. The sixth night.

And God said that it was Good.

And on the last night, God rested. And the rest was good. The rest was very good.

And God said that it was very Good.

CPSIA information can be obtained
at www.ICGtesting.com
Printed in the USA
LVHW041015210820
663704LV00004B/282

9 781848 258686